Date: 7/25/12

DOCTORS
to the RESCUE

by Meish Goldish

Consultant: Paul F. Johnston, Ph.D.
Washington, D.C.

BEARPORT
PUBLISHING

New York, New York

Credits

Cover and Title Page, © Juice Images/Alamy and Alvaro German Vilela/Shutterstock; TOC, © Corbis/SuperStock; 4, © Science Photo Library/Alamy; 5, © Paul Landsman/Dreamstime; 6, © Kathleen O'Rourke/The Stamford Advocate; 7, © Kathleen O'Rourke/The Stamford Advocate; 8T, © Adam Gault/Science Photo Library/Alamy; 8B, © Science Faction/SuperStock; 9, © AP Photo/Charles Dharapak; 10, © Harry Scull Jr./The Buffalo News; 11, © B. Bennett/Getty Images; 12, © Exactostock/SuperStock; 13, © The Canadian Press Images/Francis Vachon via AP Images; 14, © Kathy Anderson/Times-Picayune/Landov; 15T, © AP Photo/Bill Haber; 15B, © Brad Loper/Dallas Morning News/Corbis; 16, © Damon Winter/The New York Times/Redux; 17, © Federico Gambarini/dpa/Landov; 18, © AP Photo/The Baltimore Sun/Kim Hairston; 19TL, © U.S. Navy photo by Mass Communication Specialist 2nd Class Edwardo Proano; 19BL, © U.S. Air Force photo by Tech. Sgt. Dennis J. Henry Jr.; 19R, © Kim Hairston/Baltimore Sun/MCT/Landov; 20, © Julie Remy/AFP/Getty Images; 21, © Stan Honda/AFP/Getty Images; 22, © Bob Strong/Reuters/Landov; 23, © Patrick Barth/Getty Images; 24, © U.S. Army photo by Sgt. Karl Williams, 3rd BCT PAO, 1st Cav. Div.; 25, © Roberto Schmidt/AFP/Getty Images; 26L, © age fotostock/SuperStock; 26R, © Rick Wilking/Reuters/Landov; 27, © UpperCut Images/SuperStock; 28TL, © Joos Mind/Stone/Getty Images; 28TM, © Exactostock/SuperStock; 28TR, © Exactostock/SuperStock; 28BL, © Science Photo Library/SuperStock; 28BR, © SOMOS/SuperStock; 29TL, © Einar Muoni/Shutterstock; 29ML, © Radius/SuperStock; 29BL, © Rafsan Halim/Dreamstime; 29TR, Courtesy of MEDICON eG; 29BR, © Yelena Kovalenko/Alamy; 31, © Dmitriy Shironosov/Shutterstock; 32, © Ruslan Ivantsov/Shutterstock.

Publisher: Kenn Goin
Editorial Director: Adam Siegel
Creative Director: Spencer Brinker
Design: Debrah Kaiser
Photo Researcher: Picture Perfect Professionals, LLC

Library of Congress Cataloging-in-Publication Data

Goldish, Meish.
 Doctors to the rescue / by Meish Goldish.
    p. cm. — (The work of heroes: first responders in action)
 Includes bibliographical references and index.
 ISBN-13: 978-1-61772-285-1 (lib. bdg.)
 ISBN-10: 1-61772-285-5 (lib. bdg.)
 1. Emergency physicians—Juvenile literature. 2. Emergency medicine—Juvenile literature. I. Title.
 RC86.5.G65 2012
 616.02'5092—dc22
                    2011009352

For more information, write to Bearport Publishing Company, Inc., 45 West 21st Street, Suite 3B, New York, New York 10010. Printed in the United States of America in North Mankato, Minnesota.

070111
042711CGC

10 9 8 7 6 5 4 3 2 1

CONTENTS CONTENTS CONTENTS CONTENTS

Emergency!

For weeks, Dodamin Solis was having trouble breathing. He ignored the problem at first. When his feet became swollen, however, he decided to visit a neighborhood **clinic**. Doctors who examined Dodamin saw right away that something was very wrong. They rushed him to Stamford Hospital in Connecticut. In the emergency room, tests showed that Dodamin had a badly damaged heart. He needed **surgery** immediately, or he might die within hours.

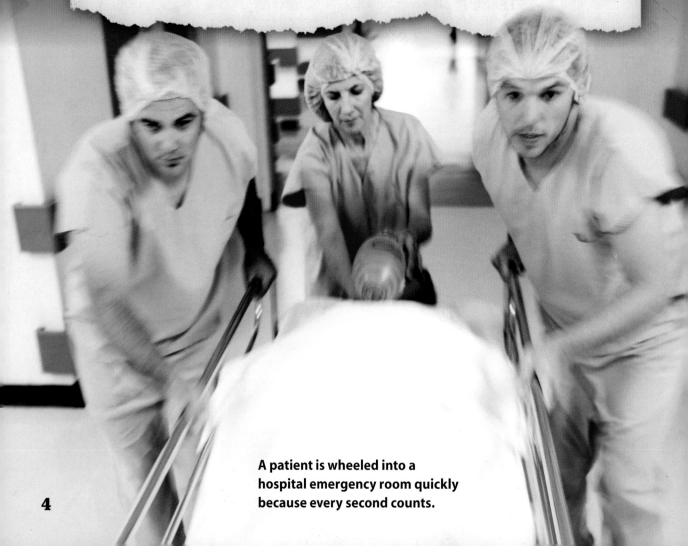

A patient is wheeled into a hospital emergency room quickly because every second counts.

Two doctors at the hospital prepared to operate. A **valve** in Dodamin's heart was leaking blood. It needed to be replaced with a new, **artificial** valve. The surgery would be dangerous. Dodamin had only a 50-50 chance of surviving. Could the doctors save his life?

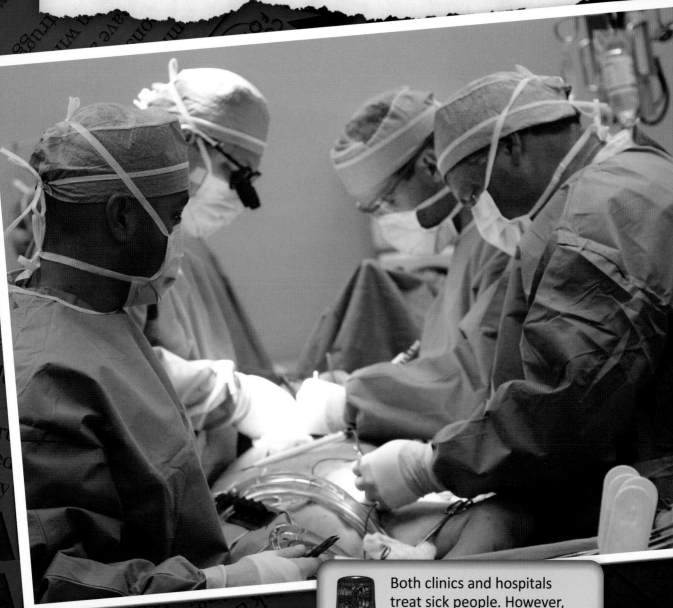

Dodamin's doctors performed his surgery in an operating room similar to this one.

Both clinics and hospitals treat sick people. However, most hospitals are larger than clinics, have more equipment, and treat patients with more serious illnesses.

A Risky Operation

Dodamin's surgery lasted ten hours. A team of nurses and other medical workers assisted the two doctors. During the most dangerous part of the operation, Dodamin's heart was packed in ice. The coldness stopped blood from flowing through his body while the leaky valve was replaced.

Dodamin shakes hands with Dr. Michael Coady, one of his surgeons.

Thanks to the doctors' speed and skill, the operation was successful. Within 24 hours, Dodamin was able to sit up in bed. Even better, he was strong enough to celebrate his 30th birthday in the hospital.

The doctors were pleased. Dr. Michael Coady said, "We're really making a difference in this community. It's the reason I'm here."

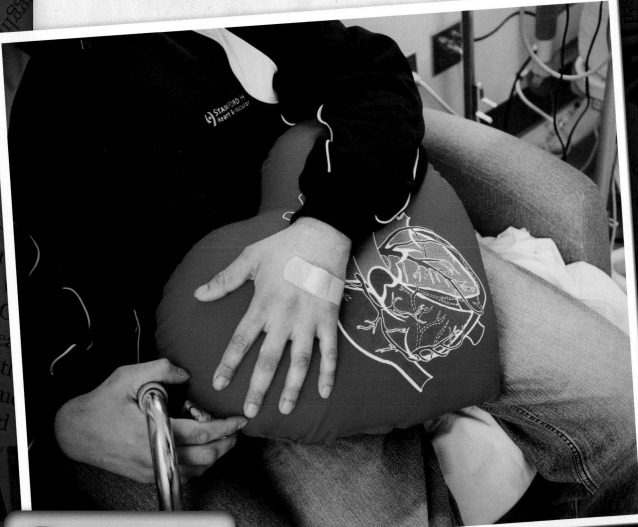

Heart surgery must be done very carefully so the patient does not bleed too much or get an **infection** during the operation.

Dodamin holds a heart-shaped pillow. After surgery, he pressed it against his chest to help him breathe whenever he coughed.

Becoming a Doctor

Dodamin's doctors were heart **experts**. Not all doctors are alike, however. Some **specialize** in other body parts, such as the brain, eyes, back, or feet. Some doctors treat specific diseases, such as cancer, or treat either very young or very old patients. Other doctors do not specialize at all. A **general practitioner** treats all kinds of illnesses.

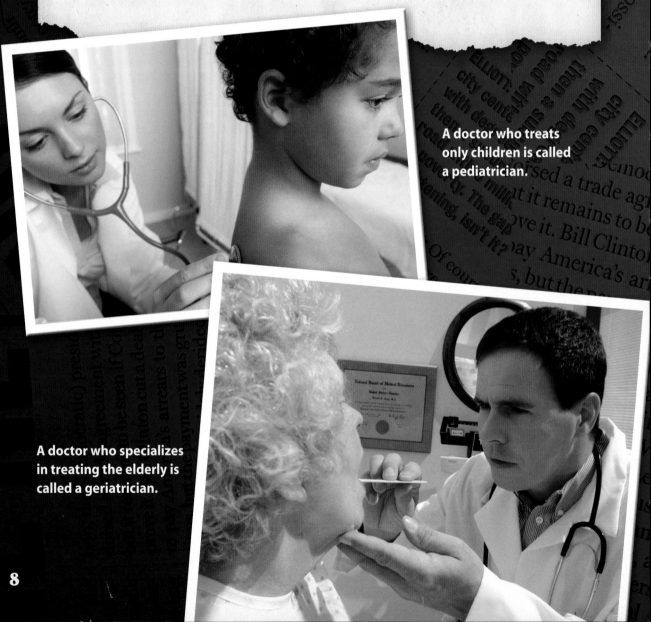

A doctor who treats only children is called a pediatrician.

A doctor who specializes in treating the elderly is called a geriatrician.

To become any type of doctor, after college, students must attend medical school. They spend two years in the classroom and two years with patients as they learn about all areas of medicine. Graduates then become **residents** who train at hospitals in their special field of interest for several more years. During that time, they become **licensed physicians**.

A resident's training can last three to eight years, depending on the person's special field of interest.

Beginning medical students learn all about the human body by studying corpses—the bodies of dead people.

Slice on the Ice

Some physicians specialize in sports medicine. These doctors treat athletes' injuries. A few of them even become the doctor for a professional sports team. They often stand on the sideline, ready to spring into action should an accident occur.

A sports doctor can be a real lifesaver. In 1989, Buffalo Sabres hockey goalie Clint Malarchuk was badly injured when another player's skating blade slashed his neck. Blood from the cut splashed all over the ice.

Malarchuk thought he was going to die on the ice as he bled.

The team's **athletic trainer** rushed to help Malarchuk. He pressed a towel against the sliced **artery** to stop the bleeding. The injured goalie was then quickly brought to the locker room, where the team's doctor, Peter James, began **stitching** the wound. More doctors helped stitch the cut as Malarchuk was brought in an ambulance to a hospital. Altogether, more than 300 stitches were needed to close the wound on Malarchuk's neck. The doctors' quick actions saved the goalie's life.

Within two weeks after his injury, Malarchuk was back on the ice and playing again for the Sabres.

A professional sports team doctor must be a licensed physician who is an expert in injuries related to that particular sport.

Baby Doctors

Can specialists save the life of someone not even born yet? Yes. Just ask Susanna Bluhm of Seattle, Washington. Susanna was six months pregnant when her **obstetrician** discovered that her **liver** was not working properly. Her baby needed to be delivered within an hour, or both mother and child would die. To save them, doctors performed an emergency surgery to remove the baby from Susanna's body.

Obstetricians are trained to perform emergency surgery when a problem suddenly arises that threatens the life of the mother or baby.

Susanna's baby weighed less than two pounds (.9 kg) at birth. For more than three months, he remained in the hospital. The baby was hooked up to machines that checked his condition constantly. Tubes ran though his nose and throat. He received three **blood transfusions**. Thanks to the hospital's baby specialists, however, he finally came home healthy.

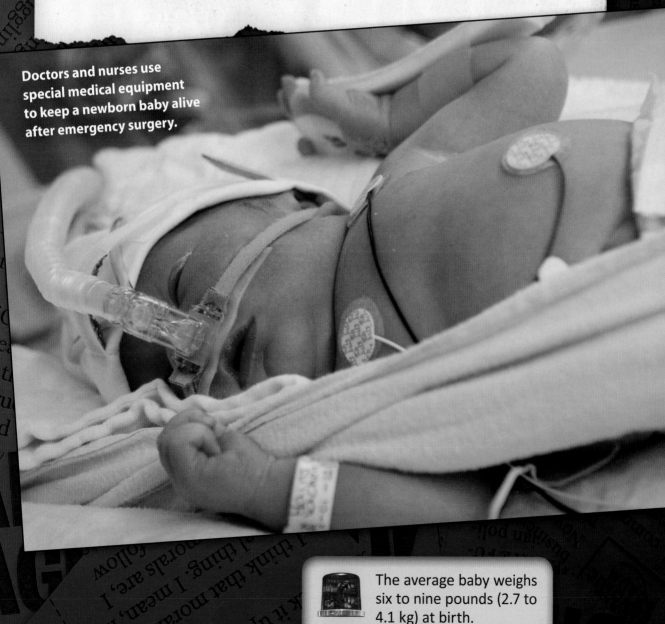

Doctors and nurses use special medical equipment to keep a newborn baby alive after emergency surgery.

The average baby weighs six to nine pounds (2.7 to 4.1 kg) at birth.

Desperate Choices

Usually a doctor treats just one patient at a time. What happens when many patients need help at once? Doctors at Memorial Medical Center in New Orleans faced that **crisis** when Hurricane Katrina struck in August 2005. The storm knocked out the hospital's power. Life-support machines stopped working. Patients needed to be **evacuated** quickly, or they would die.

Hurricane Katrina flooded the entire area around Memorial Medical Center.

Doctors realized they did not have time to save everyone. So they performed **triage**. They chose the patients with the best chances of survival to evacuate first. It wasn't easy to move the patients from the hospital, however. The streets of New Orleans had become flooded after Hurricane Katrina struck. Instead of cars and ambulances, doctors had to help patients into boats and helicopters. Luckily, more than 100 patients were still able to be rescued from the hospital.

Some Memorial patients were rescued by boat.

After Hurricane Katrina struck, the U.S. Coast Guard helped evacuate patients from Memorial Medical Center by helicopter.

Bare-Bones Surgery

An earthquake, like a flood, creates serious problems for **first responders** such as doctors. On January 12, 2010, a powerful earthquake in Haiti toppled many buildings, including hospitals. Thousands of Haitians suffered broken bones. Many victims had deep wounds in their arms and legs. If they weren't treated right away, the wounds would become infected.

Haiti's earthquake destroyed or damaged more than 250,000 homes.

Earthquake in Haiti

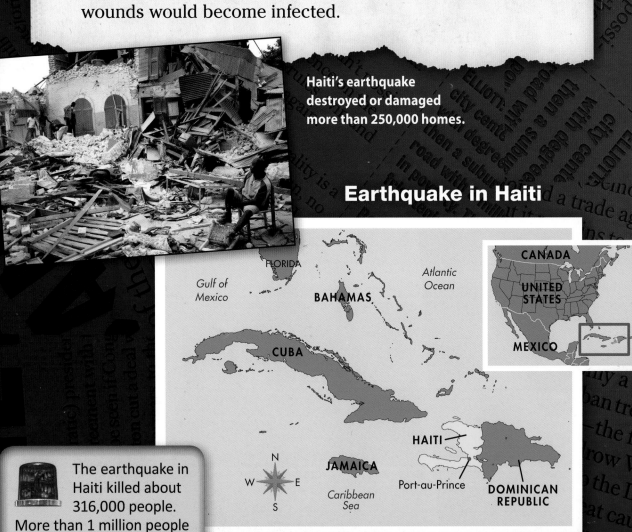

The earthquake in Haiti killed about 316,000 people. More than 1 million people were left homeless.

The earthquake struck about ten miles (16 km) southwest of Port-au-Prince, Haiti's capital. It was felt as far away as Cuba.

Unfortunately, the doctors in Haiti didn't always have the medicines they needed to stop the cuts from becoming infected. As a result, they had to cut off the wounded **limbs**. With few medical tools to work with, some doctors had to perform **amputations** with a **hacksaw**. "I call this war surgery," one doctor said. In spite of the harsh conditions, medical teams performed dozens of surgeries each day—and saved the lives of many Haitians who otherwise would have died.

Thousands of patients waited to be treated by doctors after the earthquake struck.

A Floating Hospital

After Haiti's earthquake, the United States rushed doctors and supplies to the area. A U.S. Navy ship, the USNS *Comfort*, sailed to Haiti from Baltimore, Maryland. The floating hospital was stocked with medicine, blood, and operating equipment. The medical staff on board totaled 550 people, including 13 surgeons.

The medical staff aboard the USNS *Comfort* treated patients in Haiti for more than a month and a half. During that time, doctors performed more than 800 surgeries.

The USNS *Comfort* has 12 operating rooms. It also has equipment that can produce 300,000 gallons (1,135,624 l) of clean drinking water a day.

Even before the ship docked in Haiti, many victims were flown on board by helicopter. Before long, all 1,000 hospital beds were filled. Doctors examined hundreds of patients a day. Many surgeries were performed, often to correct operations that had been done too quickly before the patients got to the ship. The doctors' skills and tireless efforts saved hundreds of Haitians' lives.

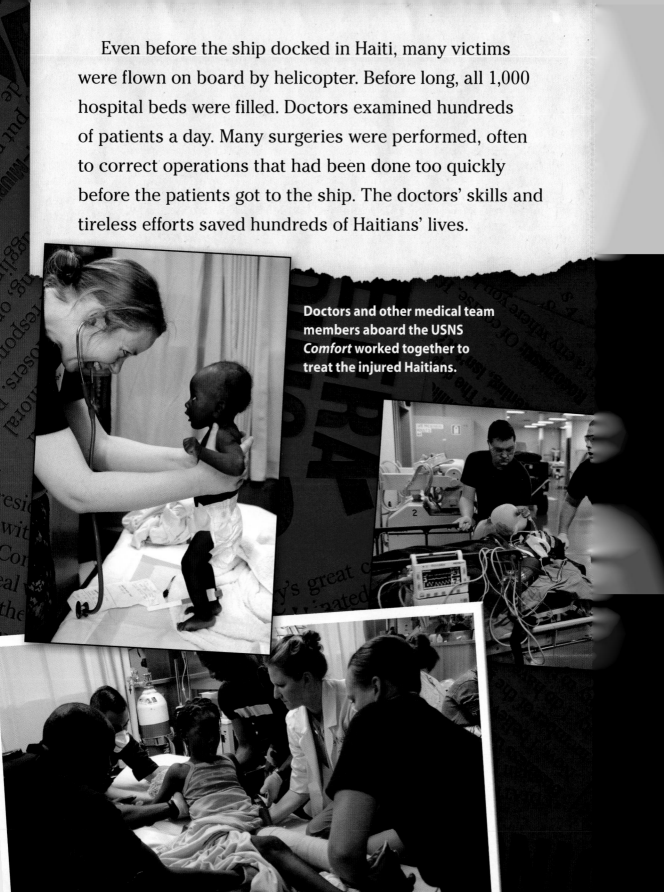

Doctors and other medical team members aboard the USNS *Comfort* worked together to treat the injured Haitians.

World Responders

Doctors from countries besides the United States also rushed to help Haiti's earthquake victims. Some responders belonged to an organization called Doctors Without Borders. This group sends physicians and supplies to places around the world where emergency medical care is needed.

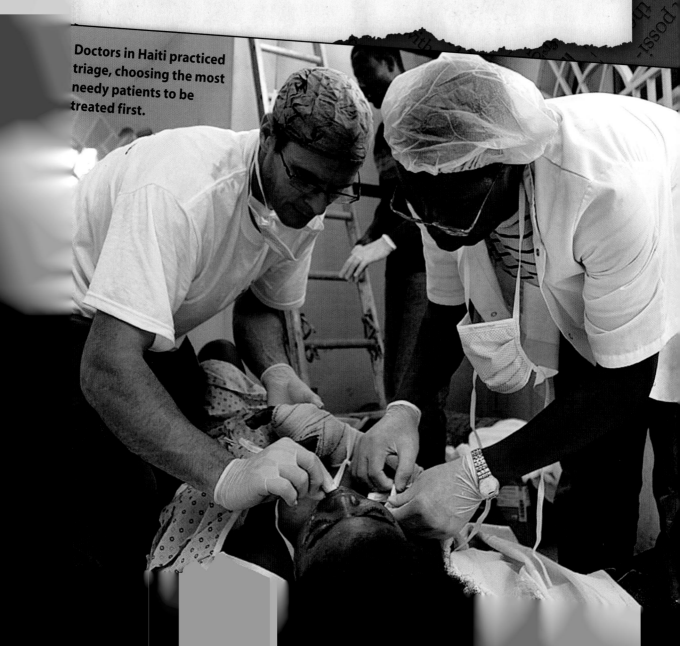

Doctors in Haiti practiced triage, choosing the most needy patients to be treated first.

Within 48 hours after the earthquake struck in Haiti, medical teams from Doctors Without Borders began arriving in Haiti. Many of them were **volunteers** who took a leave from their jobs back home to come help the victims.

So many people in Haiti needed medical help that doctors sometimes worked for 24 hours straight without rest. During their first three months in Haiti, medical staff from Doctors Without Borders treated more than 165,000 patients. By October, nine months after the earthquake struck, they had treated more than 358,000 patients, performed more than 16,570 surgeries, and delivered more than 15,100 babies.

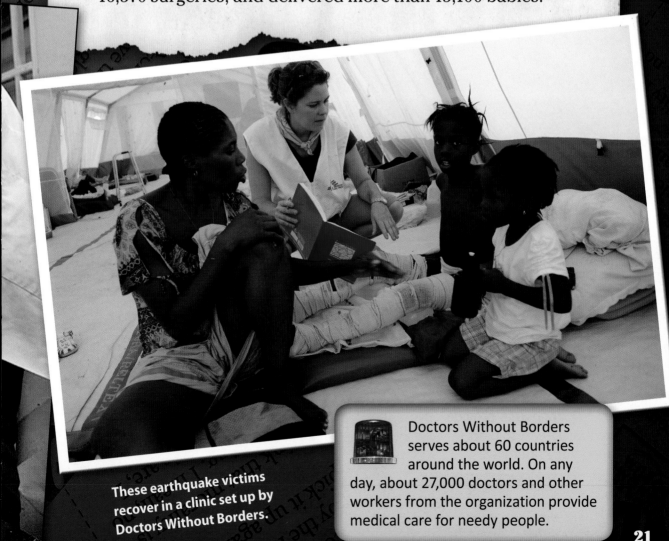

These earthquake victims recover in a clinic set up by Doctors Without Borders.

Doctors Without Borders serves about 60 countries around the world. On any day, about 27,000 doctors and other workers from the organization provide medical care for needy people.

21

On the Battlefield

In wartime, doctors are not always on the battlefield to treat injured soldiers. Instead, trained **medics** come to the rescue. Staff Sergeant John Marra, Jr., was a medic for the U.S. Army. In 2007 he aided Sergeant 1st Class Christopher Blaxton, who was badly injured by a roadside bomb in Iraq.

A medic is a valuable doctor substitute on the battlefield.

A medic is a soldier who is trained to provide medical care to soldiers in emergency situations.

When the bomb exploded, Marra grabbed his medical kit. With bullets flying around him, he inserted a tube into Blaxton's nose to help him breathe. As a rescue truck drove them away, Marra performed **CPR** and put an **IV line** into Blaxton. Thanks to the medic's skill and bravery, the soldier survived.

This medic is treating a soldier as he is being flown to a hospital in Afghanistan for more medical care.

23

Improved Methods

Sadly, many soldiers die of their war injuries. Yet in 2010, fewer American troops in Afghanistan died from their wounds than in previous years. What was the reason? For one thing, doctors encouraged medics to use **tourniquets** more often. When this device is wrapped around a wounded arm or leg, it stops the victim from losing too much blood.

tourniquet

A tourniquet presses on a blood vessel to stop the loss of blood caused by a wound.

 Today, all U.S. soldiers in Afghanistan—even non-medics—carry at least one tourniquet to use on fellow soldiers who are badly wounded on the battlefield.

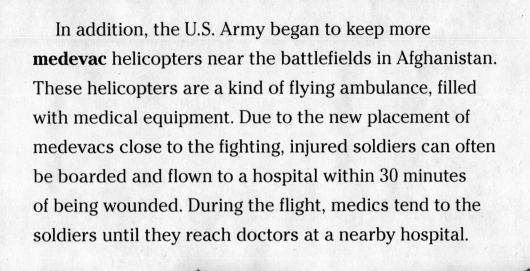

In addition, the U.S. Army began to keep more **medevac** helicopters near the battlefields in Afghanistan. These helicopters are a kind of flying ambulance, filled with medical equipment. Due to the new placement of medevacs close to the fighting, injured soldiers can often be boarded and flown to a hospital within 30 minutes of being wounded. During the flight, medics tend to the soldiers until they reach doctors at a nearby hospital.

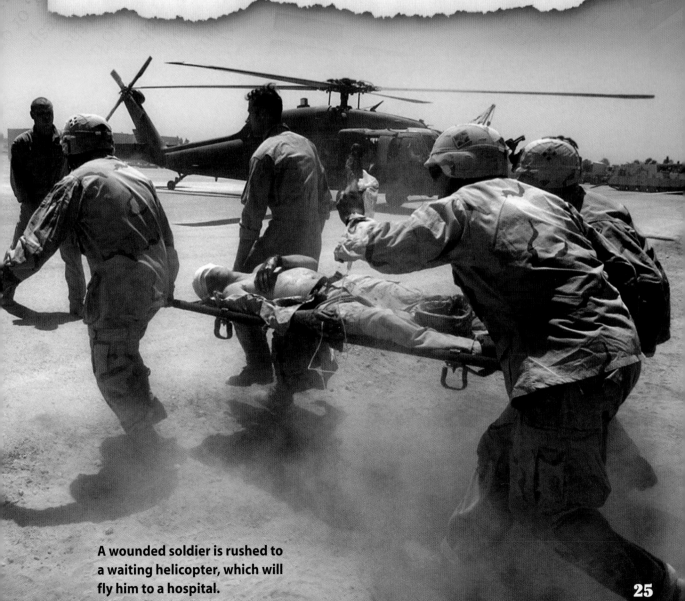

A wounded soldier is rushed to a waiting helicopter, which will fly him to a hospital.

Why Be a Doctor?

A doctor's life is hard and stressful. So why become one? As a child, Dr. Dustin Ballard of California admired Dr. McCoy, a fictional character on the TV show *Star Trek*. He liked how McCoy could easily **diagnose** illnesses. Dr. Ballard wanted to help people and make a difference in their lives—just like the TV doctor!

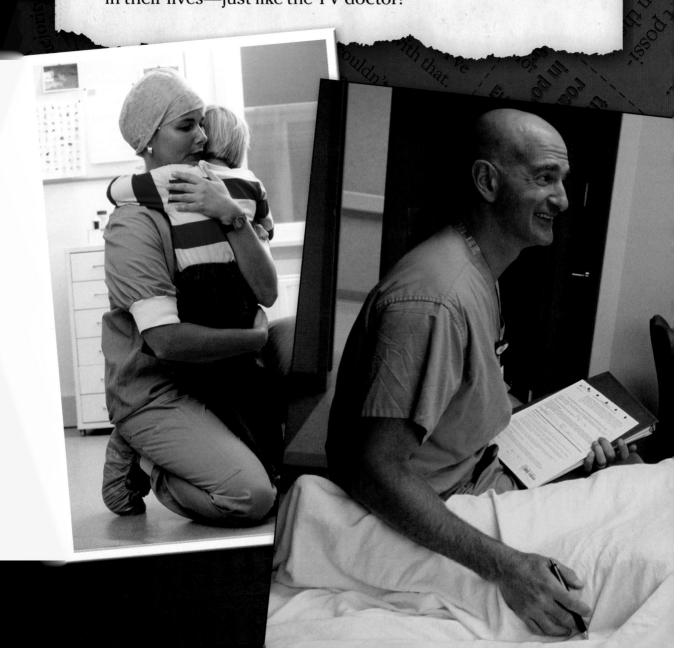

Dr. Emmeline Gasink of Virginia often travels to **remote** parts of the world where few other doctors are found. She's not just a first responder. Often, she's the only responder. Dr. Gasink visits homes, examines patients, and gives them the medicines they need. "Going door to door is what it's all about," she says. "This is why I became a doctor."

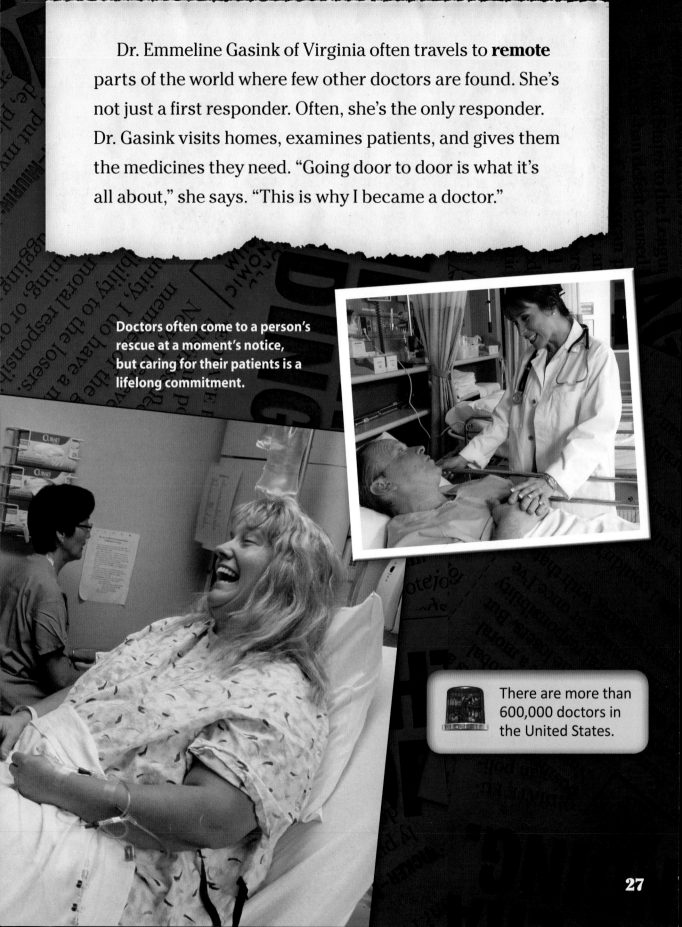

Doctors often come to a person's rescue at a moment's notice, but caring for their patients is a lifelong commitment.

There are more than 600,000 doctors in the United States.

Doctors' Equipment

Doctors use many different instruments when examining a patient.

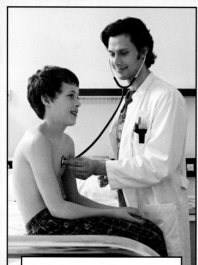

A *stethoscope* is used to hear the sounds of the heart and lungs.

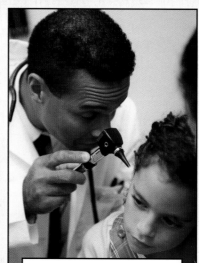

An *otoscope* is used to see inside the ears, nose, and throat.

A *blood pressure arm cuff* is used to measure blood pressure.

A *penlight* and *tongue depressor* are used to examine the throat.

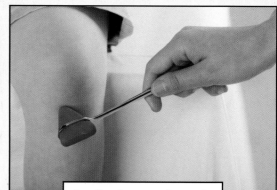

A *reflex hammer* is used to test body movements called reflexes.

Surgeons use many different instruments when operating on a patient.

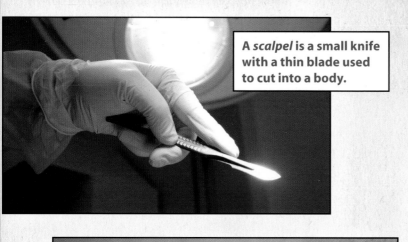

A *scalpel* is a small knife with a thin blade used to cut into a body.

A *ligature needle* passes thread around an artery to tie it off.

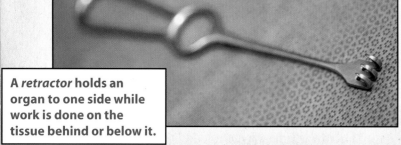

A *retractor* holds an organ to one side while work is done on the tissue behind or below it.

Forceps are used to grasp body tissue.

Metzenbaum scissors are used to cut very soft tissue.

Glossary

amputations (*am*-pyoo-TAY-shuhnz) removals of a part of the body, often an arm or leg; usually done when a body part is diseased or too badly wounded to be saved

artery (AR-tuh-ree) a tube that carries blood from the heart to other parts of the body

artificial (*ar*-ti-FISH-uhl) made by a person or machine; something not found in nature

athletic trainer (ath-LET-ik TRAYN-ur) a person who provides first aid or emergency care to players on a sports team

blood transfusions (BLUHD tranz-FYOO-zhuhnz) injections of blood into a person who is injured or ill

clinic (KLIN-ik) a building where people can go for medical advice or treatment

CPR (*see*-pee-AR) letters standing for cardiopulmonary resuscitation—a type of rescue where a person blows air into the mouth and then presses down on the chest of someone whose heart has stopped

crisis (KRYE-siss) a time of danger or difficulty

diagnose (dye-uhg-NOHSS) to determine what disease or illness a patient has and what the cause is

evacuated (i-VAK-yoo-*ayt*-id) moved away from an area because it is dangerous there

experts (EK-spurts) people who know a lot about a subject

first responders (FURST ri-SPOND-urz) the first people who come to the rescue of someone in trouble

general practitioner (JEN-ur-uhl prak-TISH-uh-nur) a doctor who treats all kinds of illnesses

hacksaw (HAK-saw) a sharp saw usually used to cut metal

infection (in-FEK-shuhn) an illness caused by germs entering the body

IV line (*eye*-VEE LINE) a tube inserted into a person's vein through which life-saving fluids, such as blood and medicine, can be given

licensed physicians (LYE-suhnsd fuh-ZISH-uhnz) doctors of medicine

limbs (LIMZ) arms or legs

liver (LIV-ur) a large important organ in the human body that cleans the blood

medevac (MED-uh-vak) a special medically equipped helicopter used to evacuate a wounded person from a battlefield

medics (MED-iks) soldiers trained to give medical help in an emergency or during a battle

obstetrician (*ob*-stuh-TRISH-uhn) a doctor who treats pregnant women and delivers babies

remote (ri-MOHT) far away from any settled place; difficult to reach

residents (REZ-uh-duhnts) people who train in hospitals after finishing medical school

specialize (SPESH-uh-*lize*) to focus on one subject or area of work

stitching (STICH-ing) sewing closed

surgery (SUR-jur-ee) the part of medical science that treats injuries or diseases by repairing, replacing, or removing parts of the body

tourniquets (TUR-nuh-kets) bandages or bands twisted tightly around arms or legs to prevent wounds or cuts from bleeding too much

triage (tree-AHZH) a system of deciding in what order sick or injured people will be treated

valve (VALV) a part of the heart that controls the flow of blood

volunteers (*vol*-uhn-TIHRZ) people who offer to do a job without pay

Bibliography

Grim, Pamela, M.D. *Just Here Trying to Save a Few Lives: Tales of Life and Death from the ER*. New York: Warner Books (2002).

Lesslie, Robert D., M.D. *Angels in the ER: Inspiring True Stories from an Emergency Room Doctor*. Eugene, OR: Harvest House (2008).

Ziegler, Edward, and Lewis R. Goldfrank, M.D. *Emergency Doctor*. New York: HarperCollins (2004).

Read More

Boyd, Nicole. *A Doctor's Busy Day*. New York: Rosen (2002).

Havelin, Kate. *Imagine You Are an ER Doctor*. Edina, MN: ABDO (2003).

Rau, Dana Meachen. *Doctors (Tools We Use)*. Tarrytown, NY: Marshall Cavendish Benchmark (2008).

Wheeler, Jill C. *E.R. Doctors (Everyday Heroes)*. Edina, MN: ABDO (2003).

Learn More Online

To learn more about doctors, visit
www.bearportpublishing.com/TheWorkofHeroes

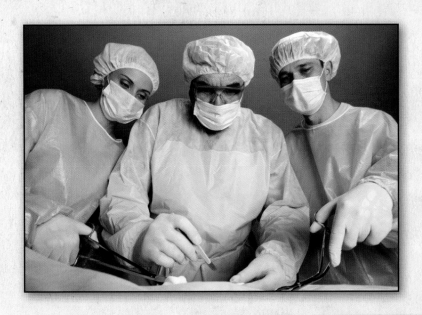

Index

About the Author

Meish Goldish has written more than 200 books for children. His books *Bug-a-licious* and *Michael Phelps: Anything Is Possible!* were Children's Choices Reading List Selections in 2010. He lives near Coney Island Hospital in Brooklyn, New York.

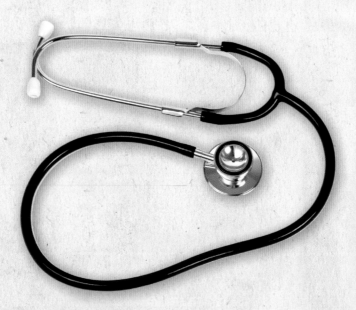